# The Birth of Our Savior Jesus Christ

As told in the Bible

Illustrated by Martha West

*The Birth of Our Savior Jesus Christ:*
*As Told in the Bible*
Text and Illustrations copyright © 2022 by Martha West
All rights reserved

**Publisher's Cataloging-In-Publication Data**

**Names:** West, Martha, author 1938-, illustrator.
**Title:** The Birth of Our Savior Jesus Christ: As Told in the Bible / illustrated by Martha West.
**Other titles:** The Holy Bible, King James Version
**Description:** Los Angeles, CA: CleanKindWorldBooks, [2022]
**Identifiers:** ISBN: 979-8-9874146-1-3 (hardback); 979-8-9874146-5-1 (softback).
**Subjects:** LCSH: Jesus Christ–Nativity. | Jesus Christ–Nativity–Art. | Christmas
**Classification:** LCC:BT315.A3 2022 | DDC: 232.92-dc23
**Audience:** Children and families.

CleanKindWorldBooks.com | 800-616-8081
2016 Cummings | Los Angeles, CA 90027 | Fax 323-953-9850
ymaddox@CleanKindWorldBooks.com

**This title is available on Amazon.com**

10 9 8 7 6 5 4 3 2 1

Printed in the United States of America

Many years ago, in Jerusalem, God sent the prophet Isaiah to tell the world of a miracle that would occur.

This wondrous event was the birth of our Savior Jesus Christ.

"... the Lord himself shall give you a sign;
Behold, a virgin shall conceive, and bear a son,
and shall call his name Immanuel."
(Isaiah 7:14)

In Nazareth, an angel came to Mary, saying,

*"And, behold, thou shalt conceive in thy womb, and bring forth a son, and shalt call his name Jesus.*

*"He shall be great, and shall be called the Son of the Highest. . . ."*

*(Luke 1:28-32)*

*"Then said Mary unto the angel, How shall this be, seeing I know not a man?*

*"And the angel answered and said unto her, The Holy Ghost shall come upon thee, and the power of the Highest shall overshadow thee: therefore also that holy thing which shall be born of thee shall be called the Son of God."*

"And Mary said, Behold the handmaid of the Lord; be it unto me according to thy word. And the angel departed from her.
"And Mary said, My soul doth magnify the Lord,
"And my spirit hath rejoiced in God my Saviour."

(Luke 1:34-35, 38, 46-47)

"Joseph her husband, being a just man, and not willing to make her a publick example, was minded to put her away privily.

*"But while he thought on these things, behold, the angel of the Lord appeared unto him in a dream, saying, Joseph, thou son of David, fear not to take unto thee Mary thy wife: for that which is conceived in her is of the Holy Ghost."*

*(Matthew 1:19-20)*

*"And it came to pass in those days, that there went out a decree from Cæsar Augustus, that all the world should be taxed."*

*"And Joseph also went up from Galilee, out of the city of Nazareth, into Judæa, unto the city of David, which is called Bethlehem . . ."*

*"To be taxed with Mary his espoused wife, being great with child."*

*(Luke 2:1, 4-5)*

Mary and Joseph arrived in Bethlehem and,

". . . while they were there, the days were accomplished that she should be delivered.

"And she brought forth her firstborn son, and wrapped him in swaddling clothes, and laid him in a manger; because there was no room for them in the inn."                                        (Luke 2:6-7)

"And there were in the same country shepherds abiding in the field, keeping watch over their flock by night.

"And, lo, the angel of the Lord came upon them, and the glory of the Lord shone round about them: and they were sore afraid.

"And the angel said unto them, Fear not: for, behold, I bring you good tidings of great joy, which shall be to all people.

"For unto you is born this day in the city of David a Saviour, which is Christ the Lord.

"And this shall be a sign unto you; Ye shall find the babe wrapped in swaddling clothes, lying in a manger.

*(Luke 2: 8-12)*

"And it came to pass, as the angels were gone away from them into heaven, the shepherds said one to another, Let us now go even unto Bethlehem, and see this thing which is come to pass, which the Lord hath made known unto us.

"And they came with haste, and found Mary, and Joseph, and the babe lying in a manger.

"And when they had seen it, they made known abroad the saying which was told them concerning this child.

"And all they that heard it wondered at those things which were told them by the shepherds.

"But Mary kept all these things, and pondered them in her heart."
(Luke 2:15-19)

It happened just as the prophets foretold in ancient times.

"For unto us a child is born, unto us a son is given: and
the government shall be upon his shoulder: and his name shall be
called Wonderful, Counsellor, The mighty God, The everlasting Father,
The Prince of Peace."
(Isaiah 9:6)

At Christmastime we rejoice that our Savior Jesus Christ was born into the world—the greatest gift ever given. And we know He will return someday as King of Kings and Lord of Lords.

Jesus, the Living Christ, is the immortal Son of God, the light, the life, and the hope of the world.

*"Glory to God in the highest, and on earth peace, good will toward men."*

*(Luke 2:14)*

# Christmas Readings Expanded

## ISAIAH:  Chapter 7

14 Therefore the Lord himself shall give you a sign; Behold, a virgin shall conceive, and bear a son, and shall call his name Immanuel.

## LUKE:    Chapter 1

26 And in the sixth month the angel Gabriel was sent from God unto a city of Galilee, named Nazareth,

27 To a virgin espoused to a man whose name was Joseph, of the house of David; and the virgin's name was Mary.

## MATTHEW:    Chapter 1

18 Now the birth of Jesus Christ was on this wise: When as his mother Mary was espoused to Joseph, before they came together, she was found with child of the Holy Ghost.

19 Then Joseph her husband, being a just man, and not willing to make her a publick example, was minded to put her away privily.

20 But while he thought on these things, behold, the angel of the Lord appeared unto him in a dream, saying, Joseph, thou son of David, fear not to take unto thee Mary thy wife: for that which is conceived in her is of the Holy Ghost.

21 And she shall bring forth a son, and thou shalt call his name JESUS: for he shall save his people from their sins.

22 Now all this was done, that it might be fulfilled which was spoken of the Lord by the prophet, saying,

23 Behold, a virgin shall be with child, and shall bring forth a son, and they shall call his name Emmanuel, which being interpreted is, God with us.

## LUKE:  Chapter 1

28 And the angel came in unto her, and said, Hail, thou that art highly favoured, the Lord is with thee: blessed art thou among women.

29 And when she saw him, she was troubled at his saying, and cast in her mind what manner of salutation this should be.

30 And the angel said unto her, Fear not, Mary: for thou hast found favour with God.

31 And, behold, thou shalt conceive in thy womb, and bring forth a son, and shalt call his name JESUS.

32 He shall be great, and shall be called the Son of the Highest: and the Lord God shall give unto him the throne of his father David:

33 And he shall reign over the house of Jacob for ever; and of his kingdom there shall be no end.

34 Then said Mary unto the angel, How shall this be, seeing I know not a man?

35 And the angel answered and said unto her, The Holy Ghost shall come upon thee, and the power of the Highest shall overshadow thee: therefore also that holy thing which shall be born of thee shall be called the Son of God.

38 And Mary said, Behold the handmaid of the Lord; be it unto me according to thy word. And the angel departed from her.

46 And Mary said, My soul doth magnify the Lord,

47 And my spirit hath rejoiced in God my Saviour.

48 For he hath regarded the low estate of his handmaiden: for, behold, from henceforth all generations shall call me blessed.

49 For he that is mighty hath done to me great things; and holy is his name.

# LUKE: Chapter 2

1 And it came to pass in those days, that there went out a decree from Cæsar Augustus, that all the world should be taxed.

2 (And this taxing was first made when Cyrenius was governor of Syria.)

3 And all went to be taxed, every one into his own city.

4 And Joseph also went up from Galilee, out of the city of Nazareth, into Judæa, unto the city of David, which is called Bethlehem; (because he was of the house and lineage of David:)

5 To be taxed with Mary his espoused wife, being great with child.

6 And so it was, that, while they were there, the days were accomplished that she should be delivered.

7 And she brought forth her firstborn son, and wrapped him in swaddling clothes, and laid him in a manger; because there was no room for them in the inn.

8 And there were in the same country shepherds abiding in the field, keeping watch over their flock by night.

9 And, lo, the angel of the Lord came upon them, and the glory of the Lord shone round about them: and they were sore afraid.

10 And the angel said unto them, Fear not: for, behold, I bring you good tidings of great joy, which shall be to all people.

11 For unto you is born this day in the city of David a Saviour, which is Christ the Lord.

12 And this shall be a sign unto you; Ye shall find the babe wrapped in swaddling clothes, lying in a manger.

13 And suddenly there was with the angel a multitude of the heavenly host praising God, and saying,

14 Glory to God in the highest, and on earth peace, good will toward men.

15 And it came to pass, as the angels were gone away from them into heaven, the shepherds said one to another, Let us now go even unto Bethlehem, and see this thing which is come to pass, which the Lord hath made known unto us.

16 And they came with haste, and found Mary, and Joseph, and the babe lying in a manger.

17 And when they had seen it, they made known abroad the saying which was told them concerning this child.

18 And all they that heard it wondered at those things which were told them by the shepherds.

19 But Mary kept all these things, and pondered them in her heart.

**ISAIAH: Chapter 9**

6 For unto us a child is born, unto us a son is given: and the government shall be upon his shoulder: and his name shall be called Wonderful, Counsellor, The mighty God, The everlasting Father, The Prince of Peace.

# Notes

# Notes

# Notes

# Notes

# Notes

# Notes

www.ingramcontent.com/pod-product-compliance
Lightning Source LLC
Chambersburg PA
CBRC090840120626
46551CB00008B/713